The Dr. Ba Cayenne Pepper Remedies Encyclopedia

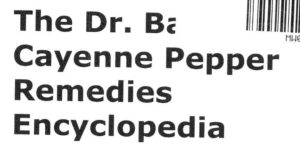

Discover Barbara O'Neill Inspired Cayenne Pepper Healing Remedies and Natural Recipes for Treatment and Curing Ailments and Boost Immune System

Elmer Hosh
Copyright@2024

TABLE OF CONTENT

CHAPTER 1

INTRODUCTION

A. Brief Overview of Dr. Barbara O'Neill and Her Impact in Natural Healing

Dr. Barbara O'Neill is highly regarded for her extensive knowledge of natural healing and her commitment to promoting holistic health practices. She is passionate about empowering individuals to proactively manage their well-being. Dr. O'Neill, with extensive experience in both traditional medicine and alternative therapies, has dedicated years to promoting the incorporation of natural remedies into conventional healthcare. She has a deep understanding of various fields, such as nutrition, herbalism, and lifestyle medicine.

With a deep commitment to sharing knowledge about the incredible benefits of natural healing methods, Dr. O'Neill has become a respected figure who motivates and guides countless individuals on their journey towards improved health and vitality. With her extensive knowledge and expertise, she has made a significant impact on individuals worldwide, helping them achieve better health and energy through her informative talks, interactive sessions, and insightful publications.

Dr. O'Neill's approach to healing is rooted in a profound appreciation for the body's natural capacity to heal itself with the right care and nourishment. She highlights the significance of addressing the underlying causes of illness instead of just covering up symptoms, promoting a comprehensive approach that takes into account the interdependence of mind, body, and spirit.

B. Welcome to the Cayenne Pepper Remedies Encyclopedia

Amidst the wide array of natural remedies, there are few substances that can match the incredible healing potential of cayenne pepper. Celebrated for generations due to its healing properties, cayenne pepper is a versatile botanical powerhouse that can help with various health issues. Cayenne pepper is highly regarded by holistic healers around the world for its numerous health benefits. It is known to support cardiovascular health, improve circulation, and possess potent anti-inflammatory and analgesic properties.

The Cayenne Pepper Remedies Encyclopedia is a valuable resource for those seeking to fully explore the benefits of this remarkable botanical ally. With the guidance of Dr. Barbara O'Neill and her extensive knowledge in natural healing, this encyclopedia provides a wealth of valuable information, profound insights, and useful advice for utilizing the therapeutic properties of cayenne pepper. C. Purpose of the Book Exploring the Healing Properties of Cayenne Pepper and Its Applications in Natural Remedies

The Cayenne Pepper Remedies Encyclopedia aims to provide readers with the necessary knowledge and tools to effectively utilize the healing properties of cayenne pepper for personal and familial well-being. This book aims to simplify the scientific aspects of cayenne pepper's healing properties and offer readers practical advice on how to integrate it into their wellness routine.

Exploring the extensive history and traditional uses of cayenne pepper will allow readers to develop a greater understanding of its significance as a healing plant. They will be taken on a thorough journey to discover the numerous health advantages of pepper, including its positive effects on cardiovascular health, digestion, pain relief, and immune system enhancement. In addition, the Cayenne Pepper Remedies Encyclopedia is a valuable tool for integrating cayenne pepper into your daily routine. Readers will find a wide range of recipes, remedies, and uses that allow them to easily enjoy the advantages of this incredible plant in different ways, such as a calming tea, a therapeutic poultice, or a tasty addition to their cooking.

Ultimately, this book goes beyond cayenne pepper and focuses on empowering individuals to enhance their health and well-being through the transformative power of natural remedies. With the Cayenne Pepper Remedies Encyclopedia, readers can gain the knowledge and tools necessary to unlock the healing potential of cayenne pepper. This comprehensive resource aims to empower individuals on their journey towards holistic wellness, fostering a renewed sense of vitality and resilience.

CHAPTER 2

Common Ailments and Cayenne Pepper Remedies

A. Respiratory Ailments

Respiratory ailments cover a broad spectrum of conditions that impact the lungs, airways, and breathing passages. From the common cold and flu to more severe respiratory infections, such as bronchitis and pneumonia, these conditions can bring about discomfort, congestion, and challenges with breathing. Luckily, cayenne pepper provides a natural and powerful solution for various respiratory issues, due to its strong antimicrobial, anti-inflammatory, and decongestant properties.

1. Dealing with Colds and Flu

Respiratory infections like the common cold and influenza, or flu, are incredibly widespread and impact countless individuals annually. Experiencing symptoms like nasal congestion, sore throat, coughing, and fatigue, these viral infections can greatly affect your daily routine and productivity. While traditional treatments primarily target symptom relief, cayenne pepper provides a comprehensive approach to easing symptoms and bolstering the body's innate immune system.

The high concentration of capsaicin in cayenne pepper gives it a spicy heat and also makes it an effective antimicrobial agent. It can help fight against the viruses that cause colds and flu. In addition, capsaicin has anti-inflammatory properties that can help reduce swelling in the nasal passages and airways, making it easier to breathe and relieving congestion. In addition, cayenne pepper has the potential to enhance blood circulation, potentially aiding the body's immune system and potentially reducing the duration of illness.

A commonly used remedy for colds and flu is tea made from cayenne pepper. To make this comforting and restorative drink, just steep a teaspoon of ground cayenne pepper in hot water, along with lemon juice, honey, and ginger for extra taste and immune-boosting advantages.

Consuming this tea multiple times throughout the day can assist in relieving symptoms, minimizing congestion, and promoting the body's innate healing abilities.

Aside from ingesting cayenne pepper, applying it externally can also help alleviate symptoms of cold and flu. Applying cayenne pepper poultices to the chest or throat can provide relief from congestion, soothe sore muscles, and induce a sense of relaxation. Similarly, incorporating cayenne pepper into a warm bath can assist in clearing the airways and alleviating muscle tension, offering respite from symptoms associated with cold and flu.

2. Throat Discomfort

Many respiratory infections, such as colds, flu, and viral or bacterial throat infections, can cause a sore throat. Experiencing pain, scratchiness, and irritation in the throat can make swallowing difficult and cause discomfort throughout the day. Although there are various over-the-counter medications and throat lozenges available for temporary relief, cayenne pepper provides a natural alternative that effectively targets the root cause of inflammation and discomfort.

The powerful anti-inflammatory properties of cayenne pepper can effectively reduce swelling and irritation in the throat. Additionally, its antimicrobial properties can aid in fighting against infection-causing pathogens. In addition, the spiciness of cayenne pepper can stimulate the production of saliva, providing a natural lubricant for the throat and offering relief from irritation.

Using cayenne pepper gargle is a highly effective remedy for soothing a sore throat. To create this effective remedy, combine a quarter to half a teaspoon of cayenne pepper with warm water and a pinch of salt. Rinse your mouth with this solution for 15-30 seconds, then spit it out. Make sure to repeat this process multiple times throughout the day for optimal results in reducing inflammation, relieving pain, and supporting the healing process.

Adding cayenne pepper to your meals and drinks can be a helpful way to alleviate sore throat symptoms, along with gargling. Including cayenne pepper in soups, teas, and other warm liquids can provide relief for the throat and alleviate discomfort. Incorporating cayenne pepper into spicy dishes can have a positive impact on saliva production and throat health.

3. Dealing with Sinus Congestion

Sinus congestion, a common condition, occurs when the nasal passages become inflamed and swollen, leading to discomfort and hindering airflow. This condition is often linked to respiratory infections, allergies, and environmental irritants. If you're looking for a natural and effective way to clear sinus congestion and promote nasal health, cayenne pepper is a great option. Unlike over-the-counter decongestants and nasal sprays, cayenne pepper provides long-lasting relief without any artificial ingredients.

The fiery spiciness of cayenne pepper is due to its abundant capsaicin content. This compound has the remarkable ability to promote blood circulation and alleviate inflammation in the nasal passages, making it a natural decongestant. In addition, capsaicin has the ability to thin mucus secretions, which can help in expelling congestion and relieving sinus pressure.

A commonly used solution for sinus congestion is nasal spray made with cayenne pepper. For this homemade remedy, combine a quarter teaspoon of cayenne pepper with a cup of warm distilled water and a pinch of salt. Transfer the solution to a clean nasal spray bottle and incorporate it into your daily nasal irrigation routine. Using cayenne pepper can effectively alleviate sinus congestion by providing a spicy heat that helps open up the sinuses and promote drainage.

Steam inhalation with cayenne pepper is a great way to clear sinus congestion and promote respiratory health, in addition to nasal spray. To enhance the flavor, consider incorporating a small amount of cayenne pepper essential oil or ground cayenne pepper into a bowl of hot water. Position yourself close to the bowl, covering your head with a towel to capture the steam. Take in long, deep breaths for a few minutes. Steam can be effective in loosening mucus and providing relief from congestion. Additionally, cayenne pepper has antimicrobial properties that can help fight sinus infections.

Respiratory ailments like colds, flu, sore throat, and sinus congestion can have a major impact on your daily life and overall well-being. However, with a deep understanding of the properties of cayenne pepper, individuals can discover relief from symptoms and enhance their body's innate healing abilities. Whether used internally or applied externally, cayenne pepper provides a safe and natural solution for various respiratory issues, promoting easier breathing and better overall health and vitality.

B. Digestive issues

Nevertheless, digestive problems like indigestion, heartburn, and irritable bowel syndrome (IBS) can disturb this delicate equilibrium, resulting in discomfort, pain, and compromised digestion. Luckily, cayenne pepper provides a natural and powerful solution for various digestive issues, thanks to its strong anti-inflammatory, digestive stimulant, and pain-relieving properties.

1. Upset stomach

Indigestion, also known as dyspepsia, is characterized by discomfort or pain in the upper abdomen that typically arises after consuming a meal. It is frequently accompanied by symptoms like bloating, gas, nausea, and a burning sensation in the stomach. Although occasional indigestion is a common occurrence and generally not a cause for concern, chronic indigestion can have a significant impact on one's quality of life and may be a sign of an underlying digestive disorder.

Cayenne pepper is well-known for its remarkable capacity to enhance digestion and provide relief from indigestion symptoms. The spiciness of peppers is due to a compound called capsaicin. This compound has the ability to stimulate digestion by increasing saliva production and stimulating gastric juices in the stomach. In addition, cayenne pepper can improve blood flow to the digestive organs, leading to better nutrient absorption and overall digestive function.

Cayenne pepper tea is a popular remedy for indigestion. To make this comforting drink, steep a teaspoon of ground cayenne pepper in hot water for a few minutes. To elevate the taste and boost your digestion, consider incorporating a dash of lemon juice and a spoonful of honey. Consuming cayenne pepper tea before or after meals can enhance digestion, provide relief from discomfort, and support optimal digestive health.

Aside from ingesting cayenne pepper, applying it topically can also help alleviate symptoms of indigestion. Applying cayenne pepper poultices to the abdomen can promote better blood circulation to the digestive organs, alleviate inflammation, and provide relief from discomfort. In the same vein, applying diluted cayenne pepper essential oil onto the abdomen can provide relief from indigestion and encourage a sense of relaxation.

2. Dealing with Heartburn

Heartburn, a prevalent digestive issue, is often described as a burning feeling in the chest or throat. It happens when stomach acid moves in the opposite direction into the esophagus, resulting in irritation and inflammation of the lining of the esophagus. If you find yourself experiencing frequent or severe episodes of heartburn, it may be worth seeking medical attention as it could be a sign of gastroesophageal reflux disease (GERD), a chronic condition.

Discover the incredible benefits of cayenne pepper, a powerful solution for soothing heartburn and supporting a healthy digestive system. Contrary to its fiery nature, cayenne pepper has the ability to alleviate heartburn by encouraging the production of saliva and the release of alkaline digestive juices that counteract stomach acid. In addition, the anti-inflammatory properties of cayenne pepper can provide relief from heartburn discomfort by reducing inflammation and irritation in the esophagus.

Adding cayenne pepper to your meals and beverages can be a helpful remedy for heartburn. Including a dash of ground cayenne pepper in soups, stews, and other savory dishes can improve digestion and lower the chances of experiencing heartburn. In the same vein, consuming cayenne pepper tea or diluted cayenne pepper juice can provide relief for the esophagus and ease heartburn symptoms.

Aside from ingesting cayenne pepper, applying it topically can also help alleviate heartburn discomfort. Applying cayenne pepper poultices to the chest or throat can promote better blood circulation, alleviate inflammation, and provide relief from irritation. Similarly, breathing in steam infused with essential oil derived from cayenne pepper can assist in clearing the air passages and relieving respiratory symptoms linked to heartburn.

3. Irritable Bowel Syndrome (IBS)
Irritable bowel syndrome (IBS) is a long-term digestive disorder that causes abdominal pain, bloating, diarrhea, constipation, and changes in bowel habits. Although the precise cause of IBS is still uncertain, various factors, including diet, stress, and an imbalance in the gut microbiome, are thought to contribute to

its development. Addressing IBS symptoms typically requires making adjustments to your diet and lifestyle, as well as utilizing specific treatments to target and relieve individual symptoms.

Cayenne pepper provides a versatile solution for managing IBS symptoms, as it possesses powerful anti-inflammatory, digestive stimulant, and pain-relieving properties. The fiery nature of this spice aids in enhancing digestion by boosting saliva production and encouraging the release of digestive enzymes in the stomach. In addition, cayenne pepper's anti-inflammatory properties can assist in reducing inflammation in the gastrointestinal tract, providing relief from pain and discomfort caused by IBS flare-ups.

One highly recommended solution for IBS is incorporating cayenne pepper capsules or supplements into your routine. These formulations include standardized amounts of cayenne pepper extract, allowing for the delivery of therapeutic doses of capsaicin without the need to consume spicy foods. Incorporating cayenne pepper supplements into your daily routine can provide valuable support for digestive health, while also potentially reducing inflammation and easing symptoms of IBS.

Alongside supplementation, making changes to your diet can also be beneficial in managing IBS symptoms and supporting digestive health. Adding cayenne pepper to your meals and recipes can contribute to improved digestion, decreased inflammation, and alleviation of abdominal discomfort. However, it is crucial for individuals with IBS to be mindful of their tolerance to spicy foods and make necessary adjustments to their intake to prevent worsening symptoms.

In addition, making changes to your lifestyle, such as finding ways to reduce stress, staying active, and staying hydrated, can also be important in managing symptoms of IBS. Incorporating stress reduction techniques like yoga, meditation, and deep breathing exercises into your routine can have a calming effect on the nervous system and provide relief from gastrointestinal symptoms. Similarly, ensuring proper hydration and following a well-rounded diet that includes fiber, fruits, vegetables, and lean proteins can help promote digestive well-being and minimize the occurrence and intensity of IBS flare-ups.

Ultimately, gastrointestinal problems like indigestion, heartburn, and irritable bowel syndrome (IBS) can have a profound effect on one's daily life and overall health. However, by incorporating cayenne pepper into their daily routine, individuals can discover relief from symptoms and promote their digestive health naturally. Whether ingested or used topically, cayenne pepper provides a reliable and natural way to support digestive health and enhance overall well-being and comfort in everyday life.

C. Circulatory problems

The circulatory system is crucial for maintaining overall health as it efficiently delivers oxygen, nutrients, and hormones to cells throughout the body while eliminating waste products. Nevertheless, a multitude of factors, such as one's diet, lifestyle choices, genetic predisposition, and underlying health conditions, can all play a role in the development of circulatory issues, including hypertension, poor blood circulation, and varicose veins. Luckily, cayenne pepper provides natural remedies that can assist in relieving these problems thanks to its powerful cardiovascular advantages, such as widening blood vessels, enhancing blood circulation, and reducing inflammation.

1. High blood pressure

Hypertension, also known as high blood pressure, is a prevalent cardiovascular condition where blood pressure levels consistently exceed 130/80 mmHg. If left untreated, it can lead to serious health complications such as heart disease and stroke, posing a significant risk. Although lifestyle changes and medication are commonly used to treat high blood pressure and support heart health, cayenne pepper provides a natural alternative that may have potential benefits in reducing blood pressure levels. Research has shown that capsaicin can help relax blood vessels and improve blood flow, promoting vasodilation. In addition, capsaicin has been found to potentially reduce systemic inflammation and oxidative stress, both of which are factors that can contribute to hypertension. Through its ability to enhance circulation and reduce vascular resistance, cayenne pepper has the potential to support healthy blood pressure levels and enhance cardiovascular function.

Adding cayenne pepper to meals and recipes can be a helpful strategy for managing hypertension. Adding cayenne pepper to savory dishes, soups, stews, and sauces can elevate the flavor profile and offer potential cardiovascular advantages. For those seeking a more convenient and standardized dosage, there are cayenne pepper capsules or supplements readily available.

Another widely used solution for high blood pressure is tea made from cayenne pepper. To make this calming drink, steep a teaspoon of ground cayenne pepper in hot water for a few minutes. Incorporating lemon juice, honey, or ginger can elevate the taste and provide additional benefits for cardiovascular health. Regular consumption of cayenne pepper tea has been shown to potentially have positive effects on blood pressure levels and circulation.

Aside from dietary changes, it is crucial to incorporate lifestyle adjustments like consistent physical activity, stress reduction, and maintaining a healthy weight in order to effectively manage hypertension. Regular aerobic exercise, like walking, swimming, or cycling, for at least 30 minutes most days of the week can have a positive impact on blood pressure and cardiovascular health. Incorporating stress reduction techniques like meditation, deep breathing exercises, and yoga into your routine can have a positive impact on your overall well-being. These practices can help lower stress hormones and promote relaxation, which in turn can contribute to better blood pressure control.

2. Inadequate Blood Flow
Restricted or impaired blood flow to certain parts of the body can result in symptoms like cold hands and feet, numbness or tingling, muscle cramps, and slow wound healing. There are several factors that can contribute to poor circulation, such as a sedentary lifestyle,

obesity, smoking, diabetes, and peripheral artery disease. If you're looking for a natural way to improve circulation and promote vascular health, cayenne pepper might just be the answer you're searching for. While medical interventions may be necessary in severe cases, cayenne pepper offers some effective remedies.

The spiciness of cayenne pepper comes from capsaicin, a compound that stimulates blood flow and relaxes blood vessels, promoting vasodilation. In addition, capsaicin has been found to have positive effects on peripheral circulation, helping to improve the delivery of oxygen and nutrients to tissues throughout the body. Through its ability to enhance circulation, cayenne pepper can effectively reduce symptoms of poor circulation and promote optimal vascular function.

Adding cayenne pepper to meals and snacks can be a great way to improve circulation. Adding cayenne pepper to salads, soups, eggs, and other dishes can elevate their flavor and offer potential circulatory benefits. For those seeking a more concentrated and standardized dosage, there are also cayenne pepper supplements or capsules available.

Regular physical activity is essential for enhancing circulation and promoting optimal cardiovascular health, alongside dietary interventions. Participating in aerobic exercises like walking, jogging, cycling, or swimming can have positive effects on blood flow to the extremities, blood pressure reduction, and vascular function improvement. Strength training exercises can also contribute to better circulation by enhancing muscle tone and supporting optimal blood vessel function.

In addition, it is crucial to make lifestyle changes like keeping a healthy weight, giving up smoking, and effectively managing health conditions like diabetes and high cholesterol to improve circulation. Ensuring a well-rounded diet that includes a variety of nutritious foods can contribute to a healthy vascular system and lower the chances of circulatory issues.

3. Dealing with Varicose Veins
Swollen and twisted veins, often appearing blue or purple, are a common

occurrence in the legs and feet. They occur when the valves in the veins become weakened or damaged, resulting in blood pooling and increased pressure, causing the veins to bulge. Although varicose veins are generally not a cause for concern, they can be bothersome and cause discomfort, pain, and aesthetic worries for certain people. Discover the incredible benefits of cayenne pepper, which can provide natural relief for varicose veins and support optimal circulation.

Cayenne pepper is known for its potential benefits in improving blood flow and reducing inflammation, which may be helpful for individuals with varicose veins. Applying cayenne pepper topically can promote better blood flow, decrease inflammation, and provide relief from the discomfort caused by varicose veins. In addition, cayenne pepper's analgesic properties can help alleviate discomfort and support vascular health.

Many people find cayenne pepper cream or salve to be a popular remedy for varicose veins. For this homemade remedy, simply combine ground cayenne pepper with a carrier oil like coconut oil or olive oil to make a paste or ointment. Massage the cayenne pepper cream onto the affected area in a gentle manner to help it absorb better. Make sure to repeat this process multiple times throughout the day to effectively enhance circulation and provide relief from varicose vein symptoms.

Aside from using cayenne pepper topically, incorporating it into your diet can also contribute to maintaining healthy blood vessels and potentially lower the chances of developing varicose veins. Incorporating cayenne pepper into your meals, beverages, or homemade remedies like teas and tinctures can offer internal circulatory benefits. For those with sensitive stomachs or digestive issues, it may be beneficial to begin with smaller doses and slowly increase their intake to prevent any potential gastrointestinal discomfort.

In addition, making changes to your lifestyle can be beneficial in preventing and relieving symptoms of varicose veins. These changes include maintaining a healthy weight, avoiding long periods of standing or sitting, and wearing compression stockings. Engaging in regular physical activity, especially exercises that focus on strengthening and increasing flexibility in the legs, can have a positive impact on blood circulation and lower the chances of developing varicose veins.

Circulatory problems like hypertension, poor circulation, and varicose veins can have a significant impact on your overall health and quality of life. For individuals seeking alternative solutions, cayenne pepper provides natural remedies that can effectively relieve symptoms and support cardiovascular well-being. By adding cayenne pepper to your diet, staying active, and adopting healthy habits, you can improve your circulation and experience more energy and overall well-being.

D. Pain relief

Discomfort is a common occurrence that can present itself in different ways and impact people from all walks of life. Whether it's due to chronic conditions like arthritis, acute injuries causing muscle pain, or the throbbing discomfort of headaches, finding effective relief is a top concern for many individuals. When it comes to treatments, many people turn to medications that may have unwanted side effects. However, there are natural remedies, such as cayenne pepper, that provide promising alternatives. Cayenne pepper is known for its impressive anti-inflammatory, analgesic, and circulation-boosting properties.

1. Arthritis

Arthritis encompasses a range of inflammatory joint disorders that bring about discomfort, limited mobility, and joint inflammation. It can greatly limit mobility and negatively impact quality of life, affecting a large number of individuals across the globe. Although there is no known cure for arthritis, it is crucial to focus on symptom management and slowing down the progression of the disease. Discover the incredible benefits of cayenne pepper, which contains capsaicin, a powerful compound known for its natural pain relief and anti-inflammatory properties. Incorporating cayenne pepper into your routine can be a great addition to traditional therapies.

Capsaicin is known for its ability to naturally relieve pain by blocking the transmission of pain signals from the nerves to the brain. In addition, it also helps to decrease the production of substance P, a neurotransmitter that plays a role in how we perceive pain. Through its unique properties, capsaicin can effectively alleviate arthritis pain and enhance joint function by targeting pain receptors and interrupting pain signals. Many people find relief from arthritis pain by using cayenne pepper cream or ointment topically. For a homemade cayenne pepper cream, simply combine ground cayenne pepper with a carrier oil like coconut oil or olive oil. Massage the cream into the affected joints to help it absorb better. For the best pain relief, it's recommended to repeat this process multiple times throughout the day.

Aside from using cayenne pepper topically, incorporating it into your diet can also be beneficial for managing arthritis symptoms. Adding cayenne pepper to your meals, teas, or supplements can offer you systemic anti-inflammatory benefits and help maintain healthy joints. For those with sensitive stomachs or digestive issues, it may be advisable to begin with smaller doses and gradually increase their intake to prevent any potential gastrointestinal discomfort.

In addition, making changes to your lifestyle, such as keeping a balanced weight, staying active, and steering clear of foods that cause inflammation, can assist in managing arthritis symptoms and enhancing joint function. Engaging in low-impact exercises such as swimming, cycling, and yoga can effectively enhance muscle strength, boost flexibility, and alleviate the discomfort often linked to arthritis. Incorporating an anti-inflammatory diet that includes a variety of fruits, vegetables, whole grains, and omega-3 fatty acids can be beneficial for reducing inflammation and promoting joint health.

2. Experiencing Muscle Discomfort

Muscle pain, also referred to as myalgia, is a frequently reported issue that can arise from various causes such as overuse, injury, tension, or certain medical conditions. The level of discomfort can vary, from mild to severe, making it difficult to move and perform everyday tasks. While rest, ice, and over-the-counter pain relievers are commonly suggested for muscle pain, incorporating natural remedies such as cayenne pepper can offer supplementary relief and aid in muscle recovery.

The active compound found in cayenne pepper, capsaicin, possesses powerful analgesic properties that can effectively alleviate muscle pain. It achieves this by inhibiting the transmission of pain signals and reducing inflammation. In addition, capsaicin can enhance blood circulation to the muscles, aiding in the removal of toxins and supporting the healing process.

Applying a cream or ointment made with cayenne pepper can provide effective relief for muscle pain. For a homemade cayenne pepper cream, simply combine ground cayenne pepper with a carrier oil and gently apply it to the muscles that need relief. Gently massage to enhance absorption and offer instant relief from muscle pain and stiffness.

On the other hand, adding cayenne pepper to warm baths or foot soaks can provide relief for tight muscles and reduce discomfort. Enhance your bath experience by incorporating a generous amount of ground cayenne pepper into a tub of warm water. The result? A truly soothing and therapeutic soak. Immersing yourself in this blend for 15-20 minutes can enhance blood flow, diminish swelling, and alleviate muscle strain.

Aside from using cayenne pepper topically or in baths, incorporating it into your diet can also aid in relieving muscle pain and promoting recovery. Incorporating cayenne pepper into your diet, whether through tea or as a seasoning, can offer valuable anti-inflammatory properties and support muscle health. However, for those with sensitive stomachs or digestive issues, it may be necessary to make adjustments to their intake in order to prevent any potential gastrointestinal discomfort.

In addition, integrating stretching, massage, and relaxation techniques into daily routines can be beneficial for preventing and relieving muscle pain. Engaging in gentle stretching exercises can be beneficial for enhancing flexibility, alleviating tension, and fostering muscle relaxation. Massage therapy, whether done at home or by a trained practitioner, can effectively target muscle tension, enhance blood flow, and alleviate discomfort. In addition, incorporating stress-reduction techniques like deep breathing, meditation, and progressive muscle relaxation into your routine can aid in muscle relaxation and enhance your overall sense of well-being.

3. Experiencing headaches

Headaches are a frequent neurological condition that causes pain or discomfort in the head or neck area. There are several factors that can trigger these, such as stress, dehydration, hormonal changes, dietary factors, and underlying health conditions. Although many people turn to over-the-counter pain relievers for headache management, there are also natural remedies available, such as cayenne pepper, that provide alternative approaches to finding relief.

Research has demonstrated that capsaicin, found in cayenne pepper, can potentially provide relief from headaches by blocking the release of substance P, a neurotransmitter associated with pain perception. In addition, capsaicin has the potential to enhance blood circulation to the brain and alleviate symptoms of headaches.

Applying a cream or ointment made with cayenne pepper to the temples and forehead can offer fast relief from headache pain. For a top-notch homemade cayenne pepper cream, combine ground cayenne pepper with a carrier oil like coconut oil or olive oil. Massage the cream onto the affected areas to help it absorb better. It's important to exercise caution and avoid contact with the eyes or broken skin, as cayenne pepper can cause irritation. Aside from using cayenne pepper topically, incorporating it into your diet can also be beneficial in managing headache symptoms. Incorporating cayenne pepper into your diet, whether through tea or as a spice in your meals, can offer valuable anti-inflammatory properties and promote the health of your blood vessels. For those with sensitive stomachs or digestive issues, it may be helpful to begin with smaller doses and gradually increase their intake to prevent any potential gastrointestinal discomfort.

In addition, making certain lifestyle adjustments like staying properly hydrated, effectively managing stress, and maintaining consistent sleep patterns can be beneficial in preventing and decreasing the occurrence of headaches. Staying hydrated by drinking water consistently throughout the day can be effective in preventing dehydration, which is a known cause of headaches. Engaging in stress-reduction techniques like deep breathing, meditation, and yoga can contribute to muscle relaxation and enhance overall well-being. Furthermore, prioritizing sufficient sleep and adopting healthy sleep habits can aid in preventing tension headaches and enhancing the quality of sleep.

Many people seek relief from pain caused by conditions like arthritis, muscle pain, or headaches. When it comes to treatments, many people turn to medications that may have unwanted side effects. However, there are natural remedies like cayenne pepper that show great potential as alternatives. Cayenne pepper is known for its powerful anti-inflammatory, analgesic, and circulation-boosting properties, making it a great choice for pain relief and promoting overall wellness. Through the inclusion of cayenne pepper in their daily routines and the adoption of healthy lifestyle habits, individuals can effectively manage pain and experience increased comfort and vitality in their everyday lives.

E. Immune system support

The immune system plays a crucial role in protecting the body from harmful pathogens, such as bacteria, viruses, and other foreign invaders. Having a robust and well-functioning immune system is crucial for staying healthy and warding off infections. When it comes to maintaining a healthy immune system, there are several factors to consider, including diet, lifestyle, stress, and genetics. However, there are also natural remedies that can help support immune system health, such as cayenne pepper. Thanks to its powerful antimicrobial, anti-inflammatory, and circulation-enhancing properties, cayenne pepper can be a valuable addition to your health routine. It has the potential to strengthen your immune system, protect against infections, and promote overall well-being.

1. Enhancing Immune System Function

An optimal immune system is crucial for safeguarding the body against infections and preserving overall health and vitality. Cayenne pepper is known for its powerful antimicrobial properties that can effectively combat harmful bacteria, viruses, and other pathogens. In addition, capsaicin has the ability to stimulate circulation and improve blood flow. This can help facilitate the movement of immune cells in the body and enhance the overall efficiency of the immune response.

Regularly incorporating cayenne pepper into your diet can boost your immune system and improve its ability to fight off infections. Incorporating cayenne pepper into your meals, teas, or smoothies can offer a range of health benefits and help boost your immune system. In addition, there are also cayenne pepper supplements or capsules available for individuals who prefer a more concentrated and standardized dosage.

Topical applications can help harness the immune-boosting properties of cayenne pepper. Applying creams or ointments made with cayenne pepper to the chest or throat can effectively boost circulation and encourage lymphatic drainage, thereby enhancing the body's innate defense mechanisms. Moreover, incorporating steam infused with cayenne pepper essential oil into your routine can assist in clearing the airways and boosting respiratory immunity.

Additionally, incorporating a well-rounded lifestyle with consistent physical activity, effective stress management techniques, and sufficient rest is crucial for supporting a robust immune system. Participating in moderate physical activity, such as walking, cycling, or yoga, can have positive effects on circulation, inflammation reduction, and immune function. Engaging in stress reduction techniques like meditation, deep breathing exercises, and spending time in nature can contribute to a sense of calm and relaxation, which can have a positive impact on immune health. In addition, focusing on getting enough restful sleep and maintaining a regular sleep routine can support a healthy immune system and enhance overall health.

2. Reducing the Risk of Infections

One of the main objectives of supporting the immune system is to prevent infections, which can cause illness, discomfort, and complications. With its impressive antimicrobial properties, cayenne pepper can be a powerful tool in safeguarding against infections and promoting overall well-being. Capsaicin, found in cayenne pepper, has demonstrated strong antibacterial and antiviral properties, making it effective against a variety of pathogens.

Regular consumption of cayenne pepper can contribute to a decreased likelihood of infections and promote a healthy immune system. Adding cayenne pepper to your meals, teas, or homemade remedies like immune-boosting tonics can offer systemic antimicrobial benefits. In addition, incorporating cayenne pepper supplements or capsules into your routine can provide specific benefits for preventing infections and enhancing overall health.

Applying cayenne pepper topically can aid in preventing infections by promoting the healing of wounds and reducing the chances of bacterial or fungal overgrowth. Applying creams or ointments made with cayenne pepper to minor cuts, scrapes, or abrasions can provide disinfection and support tissue repair. Incorporating cayenne pepper essential oil into homemade disinfectant sprays or cleaning solutions can be beneficial for sanitizing surfaces and reducing the spread of germs.

In addition, it is crucial to prioritize hygiene practices, including frequent hand washing, proper food handling, and regular cleaning of frequently-touched surfaces, in order to prevent infections. Proper hand hygiene, including washing with soap and water for a minimum of 20 seconds, is essential for eliminating harmful pathogens and minimizing the chances of transmission. Furthermore, implementing proper food handling practices, such as ensuring meats are cooked to the correct temperature and storing perishable foods correctly, can effectively reduce the risk of foodborne illnesses. It is important to regularly clean and disinfect commonly-touched surfaces in order to minimize the spread of germs and prevent infections in both the home and workplace.

3. Improving Your Overall Well-being

Promoting overall well-being and vitality goes beyond just preventing infections and supports immune system health. There are many health benefits associated with cayenne pepper, such as enhanced circulation, digestion, and cardiovascular health. It's more than just a boost for the immune system. The active compound found in it has the ability to act as a natural vasodilator, promoting relaxation of blood vessels and enhancing blood circulation in the body. Enhancing nutrient delivery to cells and tissues, supporting organ function, and promoting overall health are all important factors to consider.

Adding cayenne pepper to your meals can contribute to improving your overall health and vitality. Incorporating cayenne pepper into your meals, teas, or smoothies can add a delightful burst of flavor and offer a variety of health advantages. In addition, supplements or capsules containing cayenne pepper can provide focused support for specific health concerns or goals.

The digestive benefits of cayenne pepper can also contribute to your overall health and well-being. Its ability to enhance digestion can support a healthy gut and potentially relieve symptoms of indigestion, bloating, and constipation. In addition, cayenne pepper possesses anti-inflammatory properties that can aid in reducing inflammation in the gastrointestinal tract and promoting digestive well-being.

In addition, adding cayenne pepper to a well-rounded diet that includes plenty of fruits, vegetables, whole grains, and lean proteins can contribute to your overall health and well-being. In order to optimize your health, it's important to incorporate a healthy lifestyle that involves regular physical activity, effective stress management, and sufficient sleep. Incorporating regular exercise, implementing stress reduction techniques, and prioritizing quality sleep can contribute to a stronger immune system, a more positive mood, and increased overall vitality.

Supporting the immune system is crucial for maintaining overall health and reducing the risk of infections. Cayenne pepper provides natural remedies that can support immune function, reduce the risk of infections, and promote overall well-being and vitality. By incorporating cayenne pepper into your diet, adopting healthy lifestyle habits, and practicing good hygiene, you can support your immune system health and enjoy greater well-being and resilience against illness.

CHAPTER 3

CAYENNE PEPPER RECIPES AND APPLICATIONS

A. Cayenne pepper teas and tonics

For centuries, cultures around the world have turned to cayenne pepper for its fiery flavor and powerful medicinal properties, using it as a natural remedy for a variety of ailments. The therapeutic benefits of cayenne pepper are widely known, ranging from boosting metabolism to promoting circulation and relieving pain. One effective method of utilizing the therapeutic properties of cayenne pepper involves adding it to teas and tonics. These beverages are not only deliciously spicy, but they also offer a wide range of health benefits. Discover a variety of flavorful recipes for cayenne pepper teas and tonics, along with their many uses and potential health advantages.

1. Refreshing Cayenne Pepper Lemon Detox Tea

Ingredients - 1 cup of boiling water - Freshly squeezed juice from half a lemon - 1 teaspoon of natural honey - 1/4 teaspoon of cayenne pepper powder

Step-by-step guide

1 Boil a little water

2. Add the lemon juice and raw honey to the hot water in a mug.

3. Stir until the honey is completely dissolved.

4. Add a generous amount of ground cayenne pepper and mix thoroughly.

5. It's best to let the tea cool down a bit before taking small sips.

Uses - This invigorating cayenne pepper lemon detox tea is a great choice for starting your day or aiding in a cleanse or detox program. Using lemon juice, raw honey, and cayenne pepper together can have several benefits for the body, including alkalizing the body, aiding digestion, and supporting detoxification. Consuming this tea on an empty stomach may also enhance metabolism and increase energy levels.

Potential Health Benefits - Lemon juice offers a wealth of vitamin C, antioxidants, and citric acid, which can contribute to

bolstering immune function, aiding in detoxification, and promoting skin health.
- Raw honey provides a range of benefits, including its antimicrobial and anti-inflammatory properties. These properties can help soothe sore throats, promote digestive health, and increase energy levels.
- The active compound found in cayenne pepper, capsaicin, has been proven to have numerous health benefits. It can help boost metabolism, improve circulation, and reduce inflammation. These properties make it a great addition to a weight management plan, as well as beneficial for cardiovascular health and pain relief.

2. Immune-Boosting Tonic with Cayenne Pepper

Here's what you'll need for this recipe - 1 cup of brewed green tea - Juice of half a lime - 1 teaspoon of raw honey - 1/4 teaspoon of ground cayenne pepper - Optional a slice of fresh ginger or a pinch of turmeric

Step-by-step guide

1. Prepare a cup of green tea following the instructions on the package.
2. Add the brewed green tea to a mug, then mix in the lime juice and raw honey.
3. Stir until the honey is completely dissolved.
4. Incorporate the ground cayenne pepper into the mixture and stir thoroughly.
5. For those looking to enhance the taste and reap the benefits of a stronger immune system, consider incorporating a slice of fresh ginger or a pinch of turmeric.
6. Let the tonic cool down a bit before savoring it.

Applications - This immune-boosting tonic made with cayenne pepper can help fortify your immune system and protect against colds and flu. The combination of green tea, lime juice, raw honey, and cayenne pepper creates a powerful mixture of antioxidants, vitamins, and immune-boosting nutrients. Regular consumption of this tonic can contribute to a healthy immune system, decreased inflammation, and improved overall well-being.

Potential Health Benefits Green tea contains a variety of beneficial compounds, such as catechins, polyphenols, and antioxidants. These compounds have been studied for their potential to boost immune function, improve cardiovascular health, and decrease inflammation.

- Lime juice is packed with vitamin C, antioxidants, and citric acid, offering a range of benefits such as enhancing immune function, aiding in detoxification, and promoting healthier skin.

- Raw honey provides a range of benefits, including its antimicrobial, anti-inflammatory, and soothing properties. These qualities make it a great option for alleviating sore throats, coughs, and digestive issues.

- The active compound found in cayenne pepper, capsaicin, has been known to have several health benefits. It can help improve circulation, boost metabolism, and reduce inflammation. These properties make it useful for promoting cardiovascular health, managing weight, and providing relief from pain.

3. Digestive Tonic Made with Cayenne Pepper

Here's what you'll need for this recipe - 1 cup of hot water - 1 tablespoon of apple cider vinegar - 1 teaspoon of raw honey - 1/4 teaspoon of ground cayenne pepper - You can also add a pinch of ground ginger or cinnamon if you like.

Steps 1. Warm the water until it reaches a gentle simmer.
2. Add the hot water to a mug, then mix in the apple cider vinegar and raw honey.
3. Stir until the honey is completely dissolved.
4. Add a generous amount of ground cayenne pepper and mix thoroughly.
5. For those looking to enhance the taste and promote better digestion, consider incorporating a touch of ground ginger or cinnamon.
6. Let the tonic cool down a bit before savoring it slowly.

Applications - This cayenne pepper digestive tonic is a great option for supporting digestive health, alleviating indigestion, and aiding in detoxification. Using a blend of apple cider vinegar, raw honey, and cayenne pepper can provide benefits for digestion, inflammation, and gut health. Consuming this tonic before or after meals can enhance digestion, minimize bloating, and relieve digestive discomfort.

Potential Health Benefits - Apple cider vinegar is rich in acetic acid, probiotics, and enzymes, which may contribute to improved digestion, a healthier gut microbiome, and better blood sugar control.
- Raw honey possesses a wide range of impressive qualities, including antimicrobial, anti-inflammatory, and soothing properties. As a result, it can be highly advantageous for alleviating sore throats, bolstering immune function, and facilitating the healing of wounds.
- The active compound found in cayenne pepper, capsaicin, has been known to have various health benefits. It can aid in digestion, improve circulation, and alleviate inflammation. As a result, cayenne pepper can be beneficial for maintaining digestive health, managing weight, and providing relief from pain.
- Incorporating ground ginger and cinnamon into your diet can offer extra advantages for digestion, such as alleviating feelings of nausea, easing gas

and bloating, and supporting a well-functioning gut.

Discover the delightful and powerful potential of cayenne pepper teas and tonics, which can help you harness the healing properties of this fiery spice. Whether you want to enhance your immune system, aid digestion, or improve your overall well-being, these recipes offer a convenient and enjoyable way to include cayenne pepper in your everyday life. Through careful exploration of various ingredients and flavor combinations, you have the ability to personalize these teas and tonics to align with your unique taste preferences and health objectives. Why not add some excitement to your life by trying a revitalizing cayenne pepper tonic today?

B. Cayenne pepper poultices and salves

Cayenne pepper, renowned for its powerful healing properties, has been utilized for centuries as a natural remedy for a wide range of health issues. When it comes to external treatments, cayenne pepper poultices and salves are highly effective for relieving pain, reducing inflammation, and promoting wound healing. These topical preparations utilize the potent effects of capsaicin, the active compound found in cayenne pepper, to deliver precise relief and support the healing process. Discover a variety of easy-to-follow recipes for cayenne pepper poultices and salves, as well as their practical uses and potential health advantages.

1. Soothing Cayenne Pepper Pain Relief Poultice

Here are the ingredients you'll need for this recipe - 2 tablespoons of ground cayenne pepper - 2 tablespoons of grated ginger root - 1/4 cup of warm water - 2-3 tablespoons of flax seed meal or cornmeal - You may consider adding 1-2 tablespoons of coconut oil or olive oil as an option.
Step-by-step guide
1. Combine the ground cayenne pepper and grated ginger root in a small bowl.
2. Incorporate warm water into the mixture and stir until a paste is formed.
3. Optionally, you can incorporate flax seed meal or cornmeal into the poultice

to give it a thicker texture and improve its overall consistency.

As an expert in the field, you may consider incorporating coconut oil or olive oil into the mixture to enhance its moisturizing and anti-inflammatory properties.

5. Spread the poultice evenly over the affected area, ensuring it covers the skin completely.

6. Place a clean cloth or bandage over the poultice to secure it.

7. Allow the poultice to sit for 15-30 minutes, then gently wash off the area with warm water.

Applications - This poultice made with cayenne pepper can provide relief for sore muscles, joint pain, arthritis, and other sources of localized discomfort. The powerful duo of cayenne pepper and ginger root offers natural analgesic and anti-inflammatory properties, effectively easing pain and diminishing inflammation. Applying this poultice directly to the affected area can offer instant relief and support the healing process.

Exploring Health Benefits - The active compound found in cayenne pepper,

capsaicin, has been known to naturally alleviate pain by blocking pain signals and reducing inflammation. Additionally, it enhances blood circulation to the affected region, aiding in faster healing and decreased inflammation.
- Ginger root is packed with gingerol and other bioactive compounds that have powerful anti-inflammatory and pain-relieving properties. It has been known to provide relief from pain, swelling, and stiffness commonly experienced in conditions such as arthritis, muscle strain, and other inflammatory ailments.
- Using flax seed meal or cornmeal as a thickening agent for the poultice creates a paste-like consistency that sticks to the skin and remains in position. These ingredients also enhance the texture and help absorb any excess moisture, resulting in a more comfortable poultice to wear.

2. Cayenne Pepper Warming Salve

Ingredients - 1/4 cup of coconut oil or olive oil
- 2 tablespoons of beeswax pellets or grated beeswax - 1 tablespoon of cayenne pepper powder - Optional 5-10

drops of essential oil (such as lavender, peppermint, or eucalyptus)

Step-by-step guide
1. Gently heat the coconut oil or olive oil in a double boiler or microwave-safe bowl until melted.
2. After the oil has melted, incorporate the beeswax pellets or grated beeswax into the mixture and continue stirring until completely dissolved.
3. Take the mixture off the heat and let it cool down a bit.
4. Mix in the ground cayenne pepper until thoroughly incorporated.
As an expert in the world of peppers, you may also consider adding essential oil for a delightful fragrance and extra therapeutic advantages.
6. Transfer the salve into clean, airtight containers such as jars or tins. Let it cool and solidify completely before using.

Uses - This cayenne pepper warming salve is perfect for providing comfort to tired muscles, alleviating discomfort in joints, and enhancing blood flow. By combining cayenne pepper with warming oils such as coconut oil or olive oil, you can create a salve that deeply penetrates the skin, offering both immediate and long-lasting relief. Using this salve on the affected area can provide relief for tight muscles, alleviate discomfort, and enhance movement.

Potential Health Benefits - The active compound found in cayenne pepper, capsaicin, creates a warming sensation when applied to the skin. This can promote better blood flow, decrease inflammation, and provide relief from pain. Additionally, it has the ability to stimulate nerve endings, which can provide a counterirritant effect that helps divert attention from any underlying discomfort.
- Coconut oil and olive oil are commonly used as carrier oils for cayenne pepper. They help to dilute the spice and make it easier to apply as a salve. These oils have excellent moisturizing and nourishing properties that leave the skin feeling soft, supple, and well-hydrated.
- Beeswax serves as a natural thickening agent for the salve, resulting in a velvety and effortless application that rapidly absorbs into the skin. Additionally, it creates a shielding layer that retains moisture and hinders evaporation, thus

extending the healing properties of the salve.

3. Healing Balm Made with Cayenne Pepper

Ingredients - 1/4 cup of coconut oil - 2 tablespoons of shea butter or cocoa butter
- 2 tablespoons of beeswax pellets or grated beeswax - 1 tablespoon of cayenne pepper powder

- Optional 5-10 drops of essential oil (such as lavender, tea tree, chamomile)

Step-by-step guide
1. Gently melt the coconut oil, shea butter, and beeswax together using a double boiler or microwave-safe bowl.
2. After the mixture has completely melted, take it off the heat and let it cool down a bit.
3. Mix in the ground cayenne pepper until thoroughly incorporated.
4. You may also consider incorporating essential oil to enhance the aroma and provide extra therapeutic advantages.
After preparing the balm, make sure to transfer it into clean, airtight containers

such as tins or lip balm tubes. It's important to let it cool and solidify completely before using it.

Uses This healing balm made with cayenne pepper is a multi-purpose solution for various skin concerns such as cuts, scrapes, burns, insect bites, and minor wounds. The unique blend of cayenne pepper, coconut oil, and other soothing elements aids in the healing process, diminishes inflammation, and safeguards the skin against additional harm. Using this balm on the affected areas can accelerate the healing process and provide relief from any discomfort.

Exploring the Health Benefits - The active compound found in cayenne pepper, capsaicin, possesses antimicrobial and analgesic properties that may aid in disinfecting wounds, alleviating pain, and diminishing inflammation. Additionally, it enhances blood flow and encourages the body's natural healing abilities, expediting the recovery.

- Coconut oil and shea butter are excellent for the skin, providing deep moisturization, nourishment, and protection. They work together to maintain the skin's softness, smoothness, and hydration levels. These ingredients are packed with nutrients that nourish and rejuvenate the skin.

- Beeswax is a fantastic natural ingredient that helps to keep your skin moisturized and protected from the elements. It acts as a barrier, sealing in moisture and shielding your skin from environmental stressors. Additionally, it improves the balm's texture and stability, resulting in a seamless application and extended effectiveness.

Cayenne pepper poultices and salves are highly effective and versatile remedies that can be used to address a variety of ailments, providing relief from pain and promoting wound healing. Through the utilization of cayenne pepper's therapeutic properties and its fusion with other natural elements, these topical remedies offer precise alleviation and support for general health. If you're looking to address sore muscles, joint pain, inflammation, or skin issues, adding cayenne pepper poultices and salves to your wellness routine may provide some relief and improve your overall comfort.

C. Culinary uses of cayenne pepper for health benefits

Cayenne pepper, known for its vibrant color and intense flavor, is a versatile spice that has been a staple in global cuisines for centuries. In addition to enhancing the flavor of dishes, cayenne pepper possesses powerful medicinal properties that contribute to various health benefits. By adding cayenne pepper to your cooking, you can elevate the taste and nutritional benefits of your meals. It supports digestion, boosts metabolism, and promotes cardiovascular health. In this guide, we'll delve into the culinary applications of cayenne pepper for its potential health benefits and share mouthwatering recipes to help you enjoy its numerous advantages.

1. Enhancing Metabolism and Promoting Weight Loss

Cayenne pepper is widely recognized for its remarkable ability to enhance metabolism and support weight loss. Cayenne pepper is known for its compound called capsaicin, which has been found to boost thermogenesis, leading to increased heat production and energy expenditure in the body. Through its ability to increase the body's core temperature, cayenne pepper can aid in the efficient burning of calories and support the process of fat loss.

Adding cayenne pepper to your meals can be a simple and tasty method to take advantage of its metabolism-boosting properties. Enhance the flavors of your dishes by incorporating cayenne pepper into your culinary creations. Whether you're roasting vegetables, preparing soups and stews, or marinating meats and seafood, a dash of cayenne pepper will surely elevate the taste. Spice up your homemade dressings, sauces, and dips with a fiery flavor kick by adding cayenne pepper.

Recipe Fiery Roasted Chickpeas
Ingredients - 1 can (15 oz) chickpeas, drained and rinsed
- 1 tablespoon of olive oil - 1 teaspoon of cayenne pepper - 1/2 teaspoon of smoked paprika
- 1/2 teaspoon of garlic powder
- Adjust the seasoning to your preference

Step-by-step guide
1. Set the oven temperature to 400°F (200°C).
2. In a bowl, mix the chickpeas with olive oil, cayenne pepper, smoked paprika, garlic powder, and salt until they are evenly coated.
3. Arrange the well-seasoned chickpeas
4. Roast in the oven for 20-25 minutes, or until it reaches a crispy and golden brown texture.
5. Take out of the oven and allow it to cool for a bit before serving. Indulge in this nutritious snack or add it as a delicious topping to your salads.

2. Promoting Digestive Well-being

Cayenne pepper is known for its ability to support digestive health by promoting digestion, reducing bloating, and alleviating symptoms of indigestion. Cayenne pepper is known for its ability to support the production of digestive enzymes and gastric juices, helping with the breakdown and absorption of nutrients. In addition, cayenne pepper's warming properties can provide relief for stomach discomfort and enhance digestive function.

To fully experience the digestive advantages of cayenne pepper, consider adding it to dishes that are gentle on the stomach and easy to digest. Enhance the flavor and promote digestion by incorporating a dash of cayenne pepper into your soups, broths, and herbal teas. Lean proteins, whole grains, and cooked vegetables can be seasoned with cayenne pepper to create a nutritious and digestion-friendly meal.

Recipe Spicy Ginger Tea
Ingredients - 1 cup hot water - 1-inch piece fresh ginger, thinly sliced - 1/4 teaspoon ground cayenne pepper - 1 teaspoon honey (optional)

Step-by-step guide
1. Steep the fresh ginger slices in hot water for 5-10 minutes in a mug.
2. Take out the ginger slices and throw them away.
3. Mix in some ground cayenne pepper and honey, if desired.
4. It is advisable to let the tea cool down a bit before enjoying it at a leisurely pace.

Indulge in this comforting and digestive tea after meals or whenever you desire a comforting boost.

3. Enhancing Cardiovascular Well-being

Cayenne pepper has compounds that may contribute to cardiovascular health by supporting blood circulation, reducing inflammation, and helping to lower blood pressure and cholesterol levels. The active compound found in cayenne pepper, capsaicin, has been proven to have positive effects on blood vessels and blood flow. This can potentially lower the risk of cardiovascular diseases like hypertension, atherosclerosis, and stroke.

For heart-healthy meals, consider using cayenne pepper to add a flavorful kick to dishes that include lean proteins, whole grains, and heart-healthy fats. Add a kick of heat and a burst of flavor to your grilled chicken, fish, or tofu by sprinkling some cayenne pepper on top. For those looking to add a little extra kick and some added nutritional benefits to their meals, cayenne pepper is a great option. It can be sprinkled onto salads, added to vegetable stir-fries, or incorporated into whole grain pilafs for a deliciously spicy twist.

Recipe Spicy Black Bean Quinoa Salad
Ingredients - 1 cup cooked quinoa - 1 can (15 oz) black beans, drained and rinsed - 1 red bell pepper, finely diced - 1/4 cup chopped fresh cilantro
1/4 cup of finely chopped red onion
- Squeeze the juice of 1 lime into the mixture. - Drizzle 2 tablespoons of olive oil. - Sprinkle 1 teaspoon of ground cayenne pepper.

Step-by-step guide
1. Combine cooked quinoa, black beans, red bell pepper, cilantro, and red onion in a large bowl.
2. Combine lime juice, olive oil, cayenne pepper, salt, and pepper in a small bowl and whisk together.
3. Drizzle the dressing onto the quinoa mixture and mix until it's evenly covered.
4. Adjust the seasoning according to your taste preferences, adding more cayenne pepper if you prefer a spicier flavor.
5. Enjoy the spicy black bean quinoa salad served chilled or at room temperature for a nourishing and delightful side dish or light meal.

Cayenne pepper is not just a tasty spice, but also a valuable asset for enhancing health and well-being. By incorporating cayenne pepper into your dishes, you can enhance metabolism, aid digestion, and support heart health. Whether you're incorporating a touch of cayenne pepper into your go-to recipes or exploring new dishes that showcase this fiery spice, embracing the culinary potential of cayenne pepper can enhance your enjoyment of delectable meals that satisfy both your palate and your spirit.

D. External applications for pain relief and circulation enhancement

Cayenne pepper has a strong and intense heat, making it a popular choice for pain relief and improving circulation. When it comes to cayenne pepper, its active compound called capsaicin has gained recognition for its remarkable properties. It has the power to enhance circulation, diminish inflammation, and provide relief when applied externally. Cayenne pepper is known for its ability to provide relief for a range of external ailments, including soothing sore muscles, relieving arthritis pain, and promoting wound healing. It offers a natural and effective solution for these issues. Discover various methods to utilize cayenne pepper externally for alleviating pain and improving circulation. Additionally, find straightforward yet powerful recipes and applications.

1. Cream for Pain Relief with Cayenne Pepper

List of ingredients
- 2 tablespoons of cayenne powder
- 1/2 cup of your preferred oil (coconut or olive)
- 2 tablespoons of grated beeswax - You may also consider adding 10-15 drops of essential oil, such as lavender, peppermint, or eucalyptus, for a delightful aroma.

Step-by-step guide
1. Gently melt the coconut oil or olive oil in a double boiler or microwave-safe bowl over low heat.
2. After the oil has melted, incorporate the cayenne pepper powder and grated beeswax into the mixture.
3. Stir until the beeswax is completely dissolved and the ingredients are thoroughly mixed.

4. Take the mixture off the heat and let it cool down a bit.
5. For those who prefer, you can include essential oil to enhance the scent and provide extra therapeutic advantages.
6. Once the cream has been prepared, it should be carefully transferred to a clean, airtight container.

Usage Instructions - Gently apply the cayenne pepper pain relief cream to the affected area and massage it into the skin until it is fully absorbed. The soothing effect of cayenne pepper provides relief from discomfort, while the inclusion of coconut oil or olive oil helps to hydrate and nourish the skin. Apply as necessary for temporary relief of sore muscles, joint pain, arthritis, or other sources of discomfort.

2. Salve for Enhancing Circulation

Ingredients - 2 tablespoons of cayenne powder
- 1/2 cup of coconut oil or olive oil - 2 tablespoons of grated beeswax - 1 tablespoon of ground ginger (optional) Step-by-step guide

1. Melt the coconut oil or olive oil over low heat in a double boiler or microwave-safe bowl.
2. After the oil has melted, incorporate the cayenne pepper powder, grated beeswax, and ground ginger (if desired) into the mixture.
3. Stir until the beeswax is completely dissolved and the ingredients are thoroughly mixed.
4. Take the mixture off the heat and let it cool down a bit.
5. Move the salve into a fresh, sealed container (such as a jar or tin) and let it cool and harden completely before using.

Instructions - Gently apply the salve containing cayenne pepper to the skin and massage it into the affected area to promote better circulation. A blend of cayenne pepper, ginger, and warming oils such as coconut oil or olive oil can effectively promote circulation, alleviate inflammation, and enhance blood flow to the targeted area. Use as necessary to alleviate muscle tension, encourage relaxation, and improve overall blood flow.

3. Warming Compress with Cayenne Pepper

Ingredients - 2 tablespoons of cayenne powder
- 1 quart of warm water - Clean cloth or towel

Step-by-step guide
1. In a large bowl, mix the cayenne pepper powder with warm water to create a flavorful infusion.
2. Immerse a clean cloth or towel in the cayenne pepper infusion, ensuring it is completely soaked.
3. Squeeze out the extra moisture from the cloth or towel, making sure it's slightly wet but not soaking.
4. Place the warm, damp compress on the affected area and let it sit for 15-20 minutes.
5. Feel free to repeat the process whenever necessary to temporarily alleviate any discomfort, stiffness, or tension.

Application - The cayenne pepper warming compress is a straightforward and efficient method to alleviate sore muscles, joints, and other sources of discomfort. The warmth from the compress helps to improve blood flow to the area, while the infusion of cayenne pepper offers extra benefits for relieving pain and enhancing circulation. Use as necessary to help relax tight muscles, relieve discomfort, and enhance overall wellness.

4. Muscle Rub Made with Cayenne Pepper

Ingredients - 2 tablespoons of cayenne powder
- 1/4 cup of apple cider vinegar - 1/4 cup of olive oil - 5-10 drops of peppermint essential oil (optional)

Step-by-step guide
1. Combine the cayenne pepper powder, apple cider vinegar, and olive oil in a small bowl, ensuring they are thoroughly mixed.
2. For those who prefer it, consider incorporating peppermint essential oil to experience a refreshing and soothing effect, along with added relief from discomfort.
3. Place the mixture in a clean, airtight container like a jar or bottle for storage.

Instructions - Rub the cayenne pepper muscle ointment onto the affected area and gently massage it into the skin until it is completely absorbed. A powerful blend of cayenne pepper, apple cider vinegar, and olive oil can work wonders for relieving muscle soreness, reducing inflammation, and enhancing blood flow. The inclusion of peppermint essential oil creates a refreshing feeling that perfectly balances the warming properties of cayenne pepper. Apply as necessary to alleviate temporary muscle discomfort, stiffness, or tension.

When applied externally, cayenne pepper can provide a natural and effective solution for pain relief and circulation enhancement. If you're looking to incorporate cayenne pepper into your creams, salves, compresses, or muscle rubs, you'll be pleased to know that it possesses warming properties and powerful medicinal compounds. These qualities can effectively relieve discomfort, enhance blood circulation, and contribute to your overall well-being. By integrating these straightforward yet potent methods into your self-care regimen, you can tap into the therapeutic properties of cayenne pepper to enhance your body's innate healing abilities and experience increased well-being and energy.

CHAPTER 4

BARBARA O'NEILL CAYENNE PEPPER RECIPES FOR TREATMENT OF COMMON AILMENT AND BOOST IMMUNE SYSTEM

Barbara O'Neill, a renowned advocate for natural health remedies, frequently highlights the numerous health benefits of cayenne pepper. She emphasizes its potential to address common ailments and enhance the immune system. Here are five cayenne pepper recipes that draw inspiration from her expertise

1. Cayenne Pepper and Honey Tonic
- Ingredients - 1 teaspoon of fiery cayenne - 2 tablespoons of natural raw honey - Juice squeezed from 1 tangy lemon
1 cup of warm water
- Step-by-step guide
1. Combine cayenne pepper, honey, and lemon juice in a glass.
2. Add warm water to the mixture and stir until thoroughly mixed.
3. Enjoy this tonic at a leisurely pace to

provide relief for sore throats, alleviate sinus congestion, and enhance immune function.

2. Cayenne Pepper and Ginger Immune-Boosting Shot - Ingredients

- 1 teaspoon of fiery cayenne spice - 1 teaspoon of freshly grated ginger
- Squeeze the juice from one lemon
- Optional a pinch of turmeric
- Half a cup of water
- Step-by-step guide

1. Mix cayenne pepper, grated ginger, lemon juice, and turmeric in a small glass.

2. Warm the water without bringing it to a boil.
3. Add the warm water to the glass and mix thoroughly.
4. Consume it promptly to give your immune system a boost and find relief from cold symptoms.

3. Fiery Cayenne Pepper Garlic Soup

- List of ingredients
- 4 cups of either chicken or vegetable broth - 4 cloves of minced garlic
Dice one onion.
- Diced carrots 2 - Diced celery stalks 2
- 1 teaspoon of fiery cayenne spice

- Add salt and pepper according to your preference - Follow the instructions
1. In a spacious pot, gently cook the garlic and onion until they release their delightful aroma.
2. Incorporate carrots, celery, and cayenne pepper, and cook for a few minutes.
3. Add the broth and heat until it simmers.

Allow the soup to simmer until the vegetables reach a tender consistency.
5. Add a touch of salt and pepper to enhance the flavor.
6. Indulge in this fiery soup to heat up and strengthen your immune system during the chilly months when colds and flus are rampant.

4. Cayenne Pepper and Turmeric
Immunity Smoothie
Ingredients
One banana.
Half a cup of pineapple chunks
- 1 teaspoon of cayenne pepper - 1 teaspoon of turmeric powder
- 1 cup of coconut water or almond milk
- Optional A handful of spinach
- Step-by-step guide
2. Blend until it reaches a smooth and

creamy consistency.

3. Pour the mixture into a glass and savor this nourishing smoothie as a healthy snack or breakfast choice.

5. Cayenne Pepper and Apple Cider

Vinegar Tonic

- List of ingredients
- 1 tablespoon of apple cider vinegar - 1/4 teaspoon of cayenne pepper - 1 teaspoon of raw honey - 1 cup of warm water
- Here are the instructions

1. Combine apple cider vinegar, cayenne pepper, and honey in a glass.

2. Add warm water to the mixture and stir until thoroughly mixed.

3. Enjoy this tonic at a leisurely pace to assist with digestion, encourage detoxification, and bolster immune health.

These recipes utilize cayenne pepper in different ways to take advantage of its medicinal properties, which can help with common ailments and boost the immune system.

THE END

Made in the USA
Las Vegas, NV
08 June 2024

90897881R00046